I Am a Genius: Career Journal

The Genius

This Journal Belongs To:

● ●

● ●
YOUR NAME

GENIUS

<u>noun</u> ge·nius \ˈjēn-yəs, ˈjē-nē-əs\

A very smart or talented person: An exceptionally
intelligent or creative person, with a very great and rare
natural ability or skill, especially in a particular area.

I am

a

GENIUS

CAREER JOURNAL

By:

CANDACE COX-WIMBERLEY

This book is in celebration of the life of my dear Uncle "Jr." (Clanton Wimberley, Jr.) and Great Aunt Irene Kershaw who were great examples of unending dedication and hard work. Thank you for being tremendous individuals and passing on the entrepreneurial genes. Your love and the positive impact you have made on this universe will live on forever.

Love you.

Contents

INTRODUCTION

Working under the belief that, "you don't know what you don't know", author Candace Cox-Wimberley created the I Am A Genius Career Journal as a comprehensive workbook for individuals at any personal, professional, or educational level to own and invigorate their wildest dreams. Half-instructional, half-insightful, and completely inspirational; I Am A Genius Career Journal is the definitive workbook for cultivating the genius within.

Beginning with introspective exercises to pinpoint individual skills, desires, experiences, and opportunities for growth, the I Am A Genius Career Journal takes readers on a detailed exploration of professional options. Instead of putting the pieces together as you go, I Am A Genius Career Journal helps readers develop a solid career path and plan that aligns with their interests and aspirations.

I Am A Genius Career Journal is intended to accompany readers on a journey to set goals, seek resources, boost accountability and explore career options. I Am A Genius Career Journal is particularly useful for those who want to discover their passion, deepen their leadership skills, further their purpose, pivot into another career or embark on the first step in their professional journey. For optimal results, work through each section of the journal in a quiet space with an open mind. I Am A Genius Career Journal has been proven to be beneficial for:

- Career Centers
- Career Seekers
- Churches
- Colleges& Universities
- Community Colleges
- Entrepreneurs
- Educators
- Guidance Counselors
- Job Seekers
- Mentorship Groups
- Nonprofit & Community Organizations
- Parents
- Skills Trades Schools
- Skilled Trade Workers
- Students
- Vocational Schools
- Youth

ABModUT ME

My Name is:

My Dream Career:

Desired Salary:

My favorite college:

Highest Level of Education I will like to obtain: (circle one)
Diploma/ Skills Trade or Vocational Certificate/Associates
Degree/ Bachelor Degree/ Master Degree/
Professional Doctorate Degrees-
Medical Doctor (MD)/Lawyer(JD)/ Philosophy(PhD)/
Education (EdD)

Currently I am _____ years old

My Values:
1.
2.
3.
4.

My Interest:
1.
2.
3.
4.

My Skills:
1.
2.
3.
4.

My Talents:
1.
2.
3.
4.

My first job

Position (Title): _____

My Pay: _____

Hours worked per week: _____

What were my thoughts this job:

My first day was:

_____
_____
_____
_____
_____
_____
_____

Overall Pros:

_____
_____
_____
_____
_____
_____
_____

Overall Cons:

_____
_____
_____
_____
_____
_____
_____

My Country's Minimum Wage as of Today: _____

Today's Date:_____

ME, PERSONALLY

1. What are some of my strongest abilities?

_____
_____
_____
_____
_____
_____
_____

2. What things interest me most?

_____
_____
_____
_____
_____
_____
_____

3. What activities, people, or things really make me feel happy?

_____
_____
_____
_____
_____
_____
_____

4. What issues, world problems, or current events concern me most?

_____
_____
_____
_____
_____
_____
_____

ME, PERSONALLY

5. What are my personal strengths?

_____
_____
_____
_____
_____
_____
_____

6. What do I want to improve about myself?

_____
_____
_____
_____
_____
_____
_____

7. What is something I had to overcome?

_____
_____
_____
_____
_____
_____
_____

"The two most important days in your life are the day you are born and the day you find out why."- Mark Twain

SUBSTANTIAL P.A.A.E

Proud **A**ccomplishments
Achievements & **E**xperiences

In life, individuals are provided with internal rewards, experiences, lessons, moments and memories no one can ever take from them. These are treasures, which provide one with courage, inspiration, encouragement, endurance, motivation, strength, vision, and hope at the very moment a person may need it most.

These proud accomplishments, achievements and experiences are priceless payments to oneself in life.

What are some things in your life that have been rewarding and brought you inner fulfillment?

Thus far in my life,

5 of my **Proudest** moments?

_____
_____
_____
_____
_____
_____
_____
_____
_____
_____

"It takes courage to grown up and become who you really are."
- E.E. Cummings

SUBSTANTIAL P.A.A.E.

5 **Accomplishments** I have made?

_____
_____
_____
_____
_____
_____
_____
_____
_____
_____
_____

5 **Achievements** I have done successfully?

_____
_____
_____
_____
_____
_____
_____
_____
_____
_____
_____

5 **Experiences** I have enjoyed?

_____
_____
_____
_____
_____
_____
_____
_____
_____
_____
_____

MY GOALS

Goals

An observable and measurable end result having one or more objectives to be achieved within a fixed timeframe.

Tips for Setting Goals

1. Stretch not Stress

Your goal should stretch and motivate you, not stress you out. Set steps to accomplish your goals. Long term and short term goals will help you stayed inspired.

2. Set SMART Goals:

S – Specific

(Clearly define: Who, What, When, Where, Which, Why)

M – Measurable

(Set metrics/measurements to track of goal)

A – Attainable/Achievable

(Decide what tools are needed to achieve goal)

R - Realistic

(Be realistic, check: resources, knowledge and time)

T - Time-based/Time-frame

(Set a target date to complete goal: specific date and time)

MY GOALS

3. Stay Encouraged
Remember your goal is yours; don't allow others to discourage you. The vision was given to you, can't expect others to always understand.

4. Accountability
Have someone you trust hold you accountable. Set reward incentives for target marks you accomplish during the process. (Reward incentives can also be used if you have a partner).

5. Presentation
Write and design your goals in a layout you will enjoy looking at. The design and layout can be as creative as you will like.

6. Post & Review Often
Post your goals some place you can look at daily. This can be in multiple places (bedroom wall, screen save on phone, computer screen saver, etc.).

7. Believe
Trust and believe in yourself. Remember you can do whatever you set your mind to.

"Faith is the substance of things hoped for and the evidence of things not seen"
- Hebrews 11:1

MY GOALS

My Six Month Goals
1. ....
2. ....
3. ....
4. ....

My One Year Goals
5. ....
6. ....
7. ....
8. ....

My Five Year Goals
1. ....
2. ....
3. ....
4. ....

My Ten Year Goals
1. ....
2. ....
3. ....
4. ....

Short Term Goals:
A goal you want to accomplish relatively soon, within one year (today, this week, this month, this year, etc.).

Long Term Goals:
A goal you want to accomplish in the future, more than one year time span (in two years, in five years, in ten years, etc.)

MY GOALS

MY GOALS

My List to Help Me Accomplish My Goals

TO DO!

- [ ]
- [ ]
- [ ]
- [ ]
- [ ]
- [ ]
- [ ]
- [ ]
- [ ]
- [ ]
- [ ]
- [ ]
- [ ]
- [ ]
- [ ]
- [ ]
- [ ]
- [ ]
- [ ]
- [ ]
- [ ]
- [ ]
- [ ]

EDUCATION

FINANCE

INFORMATION
TECHNOLOGY

ARTS
&
ENTERTAINMENT

DESIGN

NONPROFIT

Exploring Careers

Career Fields

SCIENCES

COMMUNICATIONS

BUSINESS

MEDICINE

LEGAL

ENGINEERING

GOVERNMENT

i am a genius

TOP 3 Professional Sectors

Non-Profit

Associations, charities, cooperatives, and other voluntary organizations formed to further cultural, educational, religious, professional, or public service objectives.

EXAMPLES: American Civil Liberties Union (ACLU), American Red Cross, United Way, United Nations Children's Fund (UNICEF), Salvation Army, YMCA

Private

The area of the nation's economy privately controlled.

EXAMPLES: Apple, Twitter, McDonalds, Nike, Nordstroms

Public

The area of the nation's affairs controlled by the government.

EXAMPLES: military, police, public transit, public educators, elected officials

I prefer to work in the (non-profit/ public/ private) sector. Why?_____

_____

_____

MY IDEAS

STE²AM CAREERS

S-Science   T-Technology   E²-Engineering / Entrepreneurship

A-Arts   M-Mathematics

Ste²am **Careers:**

- Mathematics
- Civil Engineering
- Computer Engineering
- Computer Programming
- Environmental Engineering Technology
- Nuclear Engineering Technology
- Petroleum Technology
- Marine Sciences
- Information Architect
- Creative Director
- Graphic Designer
- Architect

As an entrepreneur you can begin your own business in any of the Ste²am Careers.

What are your thoughts about the STE²AM Career Field?

_____

_____

_____

_____

What are some additional careers in the Ste²am profession that interest you?

_____

_____

_____

_____

*Career professions are not limited to the list provided

PROFESSIONAL BIOS

Position Title: _____

Who I knew with this position: _____

Company they work for: _____

Responsibilities:_____
_____

Daily Activities: _____

Education Requirement: _____

Number of Years in school: _____

Pay Range: ___ (Entry) ____ (Median) ____ (Top)

I met this person at: _____

When: _____

Referred by: _____

Questions: _____

NOTES:

Contact Info:

Follow Up (*When*):

Rate this career: (Low) **1 2 3 4 5 6 7** (High)

Self Reflection (*My thoughts/reflections about this position*):

JOB SHADOW QUESTIONAIRE

POSITION TITLE:

What are the job opportunities for this area of work?

What kind of personal satisfaction do you get from your job?

What advice would you give a person interested in this career?

What changes do you see in this area within the next 5-10 years?

Are there any internship or co-op opportunities here at your job that I can apply for to obtain experience working in this field?

Does the company you work for offer scholarships? If so, where can I apply?

Additional Questions/Remarks:

PROFESSIONAL BIOS

Position Title: _____

Who I knew with this position: _____

Company they work for: _____

Responsibilities:_____
_____

Daily Activities: _____

Education Requirement: _____

Number of Years in school: _____

Pay Range: ___ (Entry) ____ (Median) ____ (Top)

I met this person at: _____

When: _____

Referred by: _____

Questions: _____

NOTES:

Contact Info: _____

Follow Up (*When*): _____

Rate this career: (Low) **1 2 3 4 5 6 7** (High)

Self Reflection (*My thoughts/reflections about this position*):
_____
_____

JOB SHADOW QUESTIONAIRE

POSITION TITLE:

What are the job opportunities for this area of work?

What kind of personal satisfaction do you get from your job?

What advice would you give a person interested in this career?

What changes do you see in this area within the next 5-10 years?

Are there any internship or co-op opportunities here at your job? that I can apply for to obtain experience working in this field?

Does the company you work for offer scholarships? If so, where can I apply?

Additional Questions/Remarks:

PROFESSIONAL BIOS

Position Title: _____

Who I knew with this position: _____

Company they work for: _____

Responsibilities:_____
_____

Daily Activities: _____

Education Requirement: _____

Number of Years in school: _____

Pay Range: ___ (Entry) ____ (Median) ____ (Top)

I met this person at: _____

When: _____

Referred by: _____

Questions: _____

NOTES:

Contact Info: _____

Follow Up (*When*): _____

Rate this career: (Low) **1 2 3 4 5 6 7** (High)

Self Reflection (*My thoughts/reflections about this position*):
_____

JOB SHADOW QUESTIONAIRE

POSITION TITLE:

What are the job opportunities for this area of work?

What kind of personal satisfaction do you get from your job?

What advice would you give a person interested in this career?

What changes do you see in this area within the next 5-10 years?

Are there any internship or co-op opportunities here at your job? that I can apply for to obtain experience working in this field?

Does the company you work for offer scholarships? If so, where can I apply?

Additional Questions/Remarks:

PROFESSIONAL BIOS

Position Title: _____

Who I knew with this position: _____

Company they work for: _____

Responsibilities:_____
_____

Daily Activities: _____

Education Requirement: _____

Number of Years in school: _____

Pay Range: ___ (Entry) ____ (Median) ____ (Top)

I met this person at: _____

When: _____

Referred by: _____

Questions: _____

NOTES:

Contact Info: _____

Follow Up (When): _____

Rate this career: (Low) **1 2 3 4 5 6 7** (High)

Self Reflection (My thoughts/reflections about this position):
_____

JOB SHADOW QUESTIONAIRE

POSITION TITLE:

What are the job opportunities for this area of work?

What kind of personal satisfaction do you get from your job?

What advice would you give a person interested in this career?

What changes do you see in this area within the next 5-10 years?

Are there any internship or co-op opportunities here at your job that I can apply for to obtain experience working in this field?

Does the company you work for offer scholarships? If so, where can I apply?

Additional Questions/Remarks:

RÉSUMÉ TIPS

Résumé: a short document describing your education, work history, etc., that you give an employer when you are applying for a job: a list of achievements.

Types of Résumés:

Chronological: Lists your work history in reverse order, starting with your current or most recent job and working backwards.

Combination: Blends the flexibility and strength of the other two types of resumes.

Functional: Focuses on skills and strengths important to employers. Omits specific dates, names, and places. De-emphasizes a spotty work history.

Sections to include in a Résumé:
- **Name** (First & Last)

- **Contact Information** (Email & Phone)

- **Education**
  highest level of education completed/currently in pursuit
  (name of the school or college, the degree or
  course of study, and the dates attended/graduated)

- **Work Experience** (formal job experience and any volunteer or unpaid experience you have)

- **Qualifications/ Skills**

> "Success is not what you have, but who you are."
> -- *Bo Bennett*

INTERVIEW TIPS

Job Interview:

A formal meeting in which an applicant is asked questions to determine their suitability for a particular job.

Types of Interviews:
- Screening and Phone Interviews
- One-On-One Interviews / Face-To-Face Interviews
- Candidate Group Interviews
- Panel or Committee Interviews
- Teleconferencing / Web Conferencing Interviews

How to prepare for a job interview:
Before interview:
1. Research the company/ organization.
   - Compare your skills and qualifications to the job requirements
2. Research practice questions and prepare responses
3. Prepare interview kit, include:
   - Copy of your résumé
   - Notebook for notes
   - Ink pen
   - Folder/portfolio case
4. Prepare your attire (appropriate for position)
   - When in doubt * black bottoms and white top (clean, ironed and crisp)

At interview:
1. Shake hands & make eye contact
2. Stay calm
3. Speak clearly and answer questions asked (remember to stay on subject not to talk too much)
4. Ask questions (helpful hint-can prepare questions prior to interview)

After interview
1. Follow up.
   - send a handwritten card or email to thank the representative for the interview.

INTERVIEW TIPS

5 Common Interview Questions + How to Answer Them:

- **Tell Me About Yourself**

  Prepare a pitch with 2 achievements/experiences you want the interviewer to know about and how these achievements/experiences have helped prepared you for the position.

- **What do you think is your greatest weakness?**

  Ideally this needs to be an area you are working on improving. For instance, your comfort level with public speaking may be something you're working to improve.

- **What did you like least about your last (or current) job?**

  Remember not to say anything negative about your last (current) job or employer. Maybe say you didn't have the level of growth you desire at your last (current) job.

- **Where do you see yourself in five years?**

  List your honest goals and how this position can help you achieve those goals.

INTERVIEW TIPS

- **Why should we hire you?**

  Confidently inform the employer you can get the job done; accomplish great results; and offer a great contribution to the company/team.

- **Tell me about a challenge or conflict you've faced at work, and how you dealt with it.**

  Communicate your ability to problem solve. Use the S.T.A.R. (Situation Task Action Results) method to answer this question. Discuss how you came up with a positive solution.

- **Do you have any questions for us?**

  This is the opportunity to ask questions about the position and the company. Make sure this role is a good fit for you. Also, do research about the company prior to the interview.

It is important to prepare for an interview by writing out answers to potential questions.

Then, review those answers prior to the interview.

VOLUNTEER OPPORTUNITIES

Internship:

A temporary position with an emphasis on-the-job training rather than merely employment, and it can be paid or unpaid.

Internships are offered at many companies and nonprofit organizations in various fields of work. Usually you have to inquire within the company's human resources office or on the company/organization's website.

Volunteer/ Community Service:

Work that is done without pay to help people in a community.

Nonprofit organizations offer various volunteer/community service opportunities.

Benefits of Internships and Volunteer/ Community Service Opportunities:

- Can lead to full time position
- Opportunity to learn about the position and the company
- Obtain leadership experience
- Use as a reference for future jobs
- Obtain letter of recommendation

"If you can't fly then run, if you can't run then walk, if you can't walk then crawl, but whatever you do you have to keep moving forward."
- Dr. Martin Luther King, Jr.

VOLUNTEER EXPEREINCE

Where have you volunteered?

What role did you fulfill in your volunteer experience(s)?

What did you learn from your volunteer experience(s)?

What did you enjoy most about your volunteer experience?

Additional Comments:

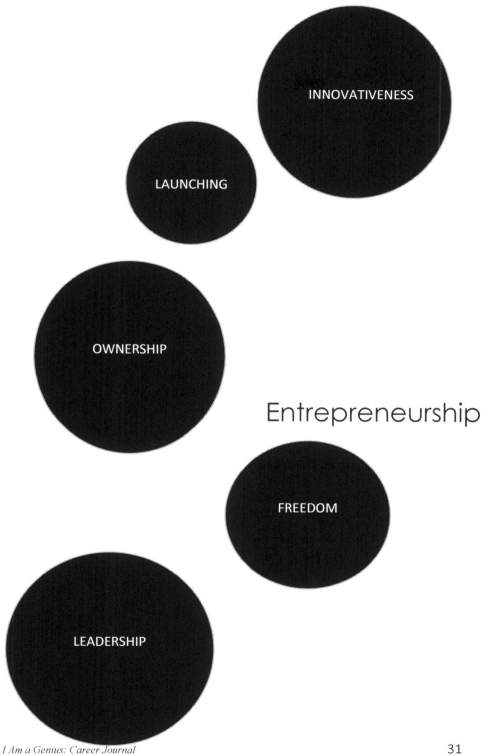

Entrepreneurship

ENTREPRENEURSHIP

Entrepreneur: A person who sets up a business or businesses, taking on financial risks in the hope of profit.

☺**Pros**: ....
....

☹**Cons**: ....
....

Names of Entrepreneurs I know	Company Name

"Logic will get you from A to B. Imagination will take you everywhere."

- Albert Einstein

SOLO
ENTREPRENEURSHIP

An entrepreneur who works alone, "solo," running their business single-handedly. They might have contractors for hire, yet have full responsibility for the running of their business.

SOCIAL
ENTREPRENEURSHIP

a person who establishes an enterprise with the aim of solving social problems or effecting social change. They drive social innovation and transformation in various fields i.e. education, enterprise development, environment, and health. They build strong and sustainable organizations, mainly with not-for-profits or companies.

ENTREPRENEURSHIP

Steps to Starting a Business:

Step 1: Write a business plan

Step 2: Get a business coach or business training

Step 3: Decide where you will operate your business

Step 4: Develop a budget and plan to finance your business

Step 5: Determine legal structure of your business

Step 6: Register a your business name with the state

Step 7: Register for state and local taxes (Get business EIN #)

Step 8: Obtain business licenses and permits (if needed)

Step 9: Understand employer responsibilities when hiring

Step 10: Use resources provided at SBA (US Small Business
        Administration)

My thoughts about starting my own business:

Entrepreneurship is the place where there is always room for
continual innovation.
–Candace Cox-Wimberley

MY IDEAS

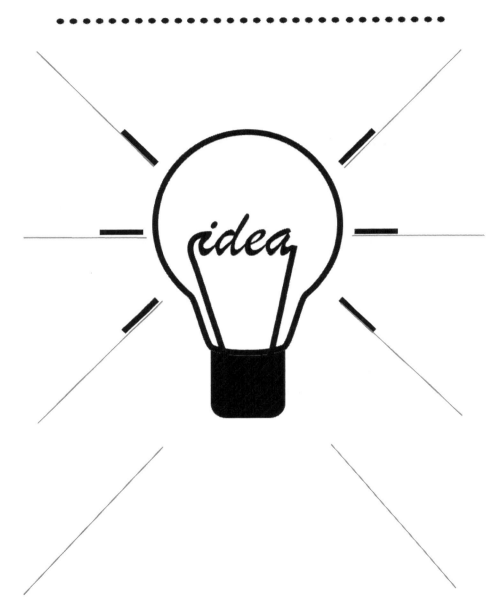

According to the National Center for Charitable Statistics (NCCS), more than **1.5 million nonprofit organizations** are registered in the U.S

Do you have the desire to start a nonprofit?
Yes or No

Why or Why not:.. ..
....
....
....
....

If you were to start a nonprofit, what would be the cause (the problem the organization would address)?
....
....
....
....

Have you ever donated to a nonprofit organization?
Yes or No

Why or Why not:.. ....
....
....
....
....

What are the names of some nonprofit organizations you like?
....
....
....
....

Steps to start a nonprofit organization?
- Decide the problem the organization will solve
- Select a name and develop the mission statement
- Recruit a board of directors of at least 3 dedicated people
- File the articles of incorporation
- Apply for exempt status with the Internal Revenue Service (IRS)
- Register with the state(s) where you plan to do fundraising activities
- Develop a sustainable fundraising plan
- Create a marketing plan to recruit donors and volunteers for your organization.

Pros:
- Ability to fulfill the need of a problem within the community
- Tax exemption/deduction eligible for federal exemption from payment of corporate income tax
- Eligibility for public and private grants
- Ability to solicit charitable tax-deductible donations
- Provide service to the community

Cons:
- High Cost: application, accountant, legal or other professional assistance
- Paperwork: annual filings to the state and IRS to keep its active and exempt status

- Shared control: laws, regulations, articles of incorporation, bylaws and board of directors
- Limited privacy: finances are open to public Inspection because of dedication to public interest

- Need for frequent fundraiser

WORK TRENDS OF TODAY

Remote Work: When an employee works someplace other than in an office (mainly from their home or coffee shops) the employee communicates with the company by email and telephone.

Working remotely is a growing trend today in workplaces.

Pros:
- Possible flexible work schedule
- Comfort of working from home
- Saves companies/organizations money (lower overhead cost)

Cons:
- Requires discipline and focus
- Limits teamwork
- Communication can be challenging
- More difficult to receive direct coaching

Does the option to work remotely interest you? Yes or No
Why:

_____

_____

Internet Integration:
- Global Business- Communication, Sales, News, Operations
- Email/Cloud- Sharing information or communication

Social Media Integration:
Social media sites are used for:
- Learning & Sharing Information
- Networking
- Learning & Sharing News
- Social Communication
- Offline Interaction
- Marketing

SOCIAL MEDIA

Some Trending Social Media Sites:

- Snapchat
- Instagram
- Twitter
- Facebook
- Youtube

- LinkedIn
- Pinterest
- Google Plus
- Tumblr
- Reddit

What are your favorite social media sites:

Do you use social media for school or work?

How has your experience been using social media?

What do you think the world would be like today if there was no internet?

What do you think the world would be like today if there was no social media?

Do you have an idea for a social media site? If so, what is it?

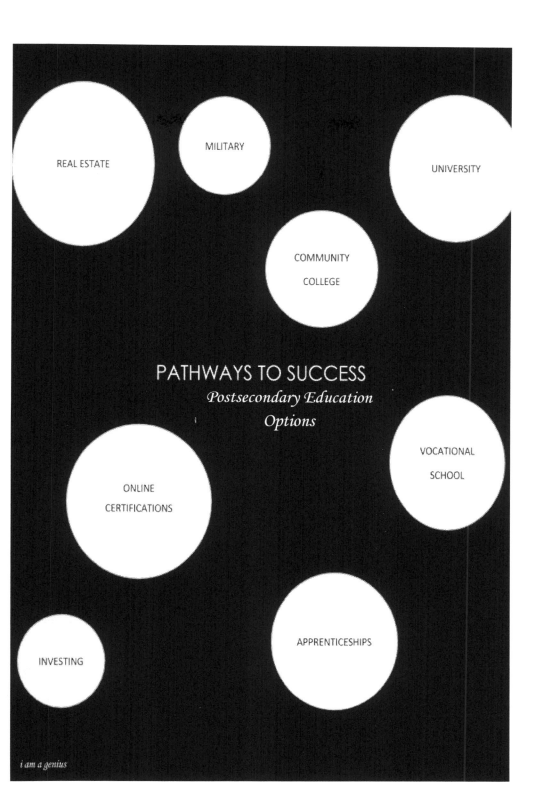

MY OPINION ABOUT COLLEGE

Do I want to go to college?
Yes or No

Why or Why not?

_____
_____
_____
_____

In your opinion, what is the purpose of college?

_____
_____
_____
_____

Do you think college is overrated?

_____
_____
_____
_____

What level of education is required for my career of interest?

_____
_____
_____
_____

Is it necessary to attend a college/univeristy in order to be Successful? Why or Why not?

_____
_____
_____
_____

I am a first generation college student: Yes or No

My mother's highest level of education:

_____

_____

My father's highest level of education:

_____

_____

My grandparent's highest level of education:

_____

_____

**First Generation
College Student**

a student whose parent(s)/legal guardian(s) have not completed a bachelor's degree. This means that you are the first in your family to attend a four-year college/university to attain a bachelor's degree.

"You've always had the power my dear, you just had to learn it for yourself."
-The Wizard of Oz

University

An institution of higher learning providing facilities for teaching and research and authorized to grant academic degrees: one made up of an undergraduate division which confers bachelor's degrees and a graduate division which comprises a graduate school and professional schools each of which may confer master's degrees and doctorates.

Degree Offered: Bachelor, Master, and Doctorate

4 Year College

an independent institution of higher learning offering a course of general studies leading to a bachelor's degree.

Degree Earned: Bachelor Degree

Community College

A nonresidential junior 2-year government-supported college offering courses to people living in a particular area.

Degree Earned: Associate Degree

Trade School/ Vocational

A school in which people learn how to do a job that requires special skills; of, relating to, or undergoing training in a skill or trade to be pursued as a career.

Degree Earned: Associate Degree/ Certification

VOCATIONAL & SKILLED TRADES

PROFESSIONS

- Construction Manager (AHP: $46.88)
- Rotary Drill Operator for the Oil and Gas Industry (AHP:$29.03)
- Boilermaker (AP: $29.16)
- Aircraft Mechanic (AHP: $28.92)
- Avionics Technician (AHP: $28.94)
- Plumber, Pipefitter, or Steamfitter (AHP: $26.49)
- Electrician (AHP: $26.73)
- Crane Operator (AHP: $26.23)
- Wind Turbine Technician (AHP: $25.50)
- Brick Mason (AHP: $24.88)
- Industrial Machinery Mechanic (AHP: $24.75)
- Plumber (AHP: $ 24.33)
- Computer Network Architect (AHP: $49.57)
- Applications Software Developer (AHP: $49.12)
- Logistics Manager (AHP: $45.74)
- Computer Programmer (AHP: $40.56)
- Database Administrator (AHP: $40.51)
- Funeral Service Manager (AHP: $40.61)
- Film or Video Editor (AHP: $38.61)
- Fashion Designer (AHP: $35.18)
- Dental Hygienist (AHP: $34.96)
- Multimedia Artist or Animator (AHP: $33.80)
- Web Developer (AHP: 33.97)
- Sound Engineering Technician (AHP: $30.45)
- Commercial Pilot (AHP: $36.61)
- Paralegal/Legal Assistant (AHP: $23.47)
- Flight Attendant (AHP: $ 18.32)

COSMOTOLOGY PROFESSIONS

Hairstylist, Barber, Hair Color Specialist, Nail Technician, Makeup Artist, Massage Therapist

* AHP- Average Hourly Pay (pay rates can vary)
**All skilled trade and vocational careers are not listed

REFLECTIONS

This section is designed to write your thoughts about your work experiences and lessons learned from this career journal. It is also suitable for writing reflections for an internship program, youth job program or new job.

Below are some questions and topics to consider while writing your reflections:

- What skills or talents did you discover about yourself as your completed this journal or during your work experience?
- What creative ideas did you contribute to the company?
- What difficulties or challenges did you encounter? How did you handle the situation?
- What were your learning objectives? Did you succeed in meeting them?
- Describe the working style you embodied: assertive, responsible, inquisitive, patient, etc.
- How does your experience relate to what you want to do after graduation?(if applicable)
- How did you deal with coaching and criticism? What did you learn from your mistakes?
- What was the organizational culture– dress, level of formality, physical office structure, staff meetings, hierarchy, worker input in decision-making, values, or reward system.
- What feedback did you receive about your performance?
- What changes did you see in yourself or the organization as a result of your experience?
- What was the management style of your supervisor? What type of style do you prefer and why?
- What insights of the professional work world have you gained as a result of your experience?
- What did you value most about your experience? Would you recommend this experience to others?
- Prepare an "elevator speech" (30 second statement) that you could use to tell others about your experience.

REFLECTIONS

REFLECTIONS

REFLECTIONS

_____

_____

_____

_____

_____

_____

_____

_____

_____

_____

_____

_____

_____

_____

_____

_____

_____

_____

_____

_____

_____

REFLECTIONS

_____

_____

_____

_____

_____

_____

_____

_____

_____

_____

_____

_____

_____

_____

_____

_____

_____

_____

_____

_____

_____

NOTES

NOTES

NOTES

NOTES

CONTACTS

Name:
Company: Title:
Email:
Phone (mobile)   (Work):
Address:
City: State: Zip:

Name:
Company: Title:
Email:
Phone (mobile)   (Work):
Address:
City: State: Zip:

Name:
Company: Title:
Email:
Phone (mobile)   (Work):
Address:
City: State: Zip:

Name:
Company: Title:
Email:
Phone (mobile)   (Work):
Address:
City: State: Zip:

CONTACTS

Name:
Company: Title:
Email:
Phone (mobile)   (Work):
Address:
City: State: Zip:

Name:
Company: Title:
 Email:
Phone (mobile)   (Work):
Address:
City: State: Zip:

Name:
Company: Title:
Email:
Phone (mobile)   (Work):
Address:
City: State: Zip:

Name:
Company: Title:
Email:
Phone (mobile)   (Work):
Address:
City: State: Zip:

CONTACTS

Name: _____
Company: _____ Title: _____
Email: _____
Phone (mobile) _____ (Work): _____
Address: _____
City: _____ State: _____ Zip: _____

Name: _____
Company: _____ Title: _____
Email: _____
Phone (mobile) _____ (Work): _____
Address: _____
City: _____ State: _____ Zip: _____

Name: _____
Company: _____ Title: _____
 Email: _____
Phone (mobile) _____ (Work): _____
Address: _____
City: _____ State: _____ Zip: _____

Name: _____
Company: _____ Title: _____
 Email: _____
Phone (mobile) _____ (Work): _____
Address: _____
City: _____ State:____ Zip: _____

CONTACTS

Name:
Company: Title:
Email:
Phone (mobile)   (Work):
Address:
City: State: Zip:

Name:
Company: Title:
Email:
Phone (mobile)   (Work):
Address:
City: State: Zip:

Name:
Company: Title:
Email:
Phone (mobile)   (Work):
Address:
City: State: Zip:

Name:
Company: Title:
Email:
Phone (mobile)   (Work):
Address:
City: State: Zip:

CONTACTS

Name:
Company: _____ Title: _____
Email:
Phone (mobile) _____ (Work): _____
Address: _____
City: _____ State: _____ Zip: _____

Name:
Company: _____ Title: _____
Email:
Phone (mobile) _____ (Work): _____
Address: _____
City: _____ State: _____ Zip: _____

Name:
Company: _____ Title: _____
Email:
Phone (mobile) _____ (Work): _____
Address: _____
City: _____ State: _____ Zip: _____

Name:
Company: _____ Title: _____
Email:
Phone (mobile) _____ (Work): _____
Address: _____
City: _____ State: _____ Zip: _____

YEAR_____

January
S	M	T	W	T	F	S

February
S	M	T	W	T	F	S

March
S	M	T	W	T	F	S

April
S	M	T	W	T	F	S

May
S	M	T	W	T	F	S

June
S	M	T	W	T	F	S

July
S	M	T	W	T	F	S

August
S	M	T	W	T	F	S

September
S	M	T	W	T	F	S

October
S	M	T	W	T	F	S

November
S	M	T	W	T	F	S

December
S	M	T	W	T	F	S

NOTES:

_____

_____

_____

MOMENTS OF GRATITUDE

Dear God, thank you for your unconditional love for me and for being with me every step of the way. I am grateful for the beautiful gifts you have provided me with in my journey of life that has come in multiple forms. I am especially grateful for the individuals who have made my journey a joyous one.

Mom, Venus Wimberley, thank you for being all of who you are. Your support, love, gentleness, sacrifices and giving heart has greatly shaped the woman who I am today. Thank you for always believing in me and motivating me to be the very best version of myself. I love you more than words will ever be able to describe.

Sweets (my grandparents), thank you for the wealth of deeply rooted love you have provided to me and our family. The moments created with you give birth to a lifetime of refreshing memories.

Bishop Charles and Lady Crisette Ellis thank you both for being instrumental role models and influential leaders. I thank you and my Greater Grace Temple church family for all of the love and support you have given throughout my life.

To all of my family, friends and loved ones, I treasure the positive contributions you are to my life. Greg Reed, thank you for being an incredibly inspiring mentor.

My city of "Detroit" and the community, educators, youth, and local businesses, thank you for your heartfelt belief and support. I thank each and every Ingenuity participant for believing in the mission and taking the time to invest in yourselves.

Candace, thank you for the courage, faith, acts of serenity, strength you have devoted to pressing forward and helping others.

All of my fellow entrepreneurs, thank you for having heart, taking risk, having faith and allowing innovative creativity to pulse through you. May we lean on each other for a natural flow of support as a reminder to keep going, start again when necessary and never give up.

ABOUT THE AUTHOR

From the outside looking in, Candace Cox-Wimberley is a gracious go-getter, an enlightened entrepreneur, a proud author, and the spirit-filled CEO of Ingenuity College Preparatory Inst., LLC. Whether mentoring the girl next door or spearheading international environmental reform, Candace is the embodiment of poise and passion. As a fierce youth advocate, internationally acclaimed motivational speaker and gifted leader, Candace believes that the best successes are meant to be shared.

What's her secret? She works from the inside out.

Throughout her proud Detroit upbringing, Candace encountered and enhanced a series of tight-knit communities. Her role with the city of Detroit in the 7th grade jump-started Candace's interest in civic engagement. After graduating from the illustrious Cass Technical High School, Candace graduated from Michigan State University with a degree in human services. Upon graduation, Candace furthered her knowledge in graduate school at University of Michigan where she studied public administration. Drawing from her exceptional ability to manage people and projects, Candace secured a role with the Michigan House of Representatives directly after college. She uses her experiences of working with nationally recognized brands like Ford, General Motors and United Way to teach others about the public, private and nonprofit sectors.

Ready to follow her lead? Not so fast, she would rather walk the path with you.

Candace's most cherished moments are spent as she encourages entrepreneurship, explores post-secondary options, skill trades, life skills and college readiness with youth. Through unwavering dedication and insight, Candace has become a sought-after resource for schools, colleges and universities around the world. She has been a featured guest on national television and radio outlets including PBS.

Candace founded I Am A Genius, an inspirational brand that motivates individuals to cultivate the genius within. I Am A Genius' inaugural mentorship program, Young Ladies Finding Their Genius Within, supports young ladies with goal setting, building healthy self-esteem and the development of entrepreneurship skill sets. Candace's I Am A Genius imprint includes apparel, mentorship programming, training workshops and speaking engagements. Candace Cox-Wimberley wields her razor-sharp focus as a tool instead of a weapon, drawing others near and guiding them toward their divine purpose. In a word, she is ingenious.

CONNECT WITH CANDACE

To request Candace Cox-Wimberley

for speaking engagements, media interviews,

or to place bulk book orders

please email: info@iamagenius.net

Website: www.iamagenius.net

Social Media:

#iamagenius

.

References

http://www.merriam-webster.com/dictionary/genius | https://en.oxforddictionaries.com/definition/genius | http://dictionary.cambridge.org/us/dictionary/english/genius
http://www.businessdictionary.com/definition/goal.html | http://www.businessdictionary.com/definition/non-profit-organization-NPO.html | http://www.dictionary.com/browse/private-sector
| http://www.dictionary.com/browse/public-sector | http://www.merriam-webster.com/dictionary/interview | https://en.oxforddictionaries.com/definition/job_interview |
https://www.careerwise.mnscu.edu/jobs/resumecharts.html | https://en.oxforddictionaries.com/definition/social_entrepreneur | http://www.trade-schools.net/articles/trade-school-jobs.asp
| http://www.businessdictionary.com/definition/vocational-training.html |

Companies and organizations listed are for use of example and not endorsement.

Made in the USA
Middletown, DE
21 May 2017